Life Without Jargon

How to help people with learning difficulties
understand what you are saying

by Virginia Moffatt

Choice Press

Cataloguing in publication data

A catalogue record for this book is available from the British Library

Published by Choice Press

Choice Consultancy Services Ltd.

27 Barry Road, East Dulwich, London SE22 0HX

Tel. 0181 299 3030; Fax. 0181 299 4500

© Southwark Consortium, 1996

First edition 1996

Illustrations by Tom Moffatt

Typeset by Paul Hutton

Printed and bound in Great Britain by HMSO, Edinburgh

ISBN 1-900532-01-8

This book is dedicated to the memory of my father, Joseph Henry Moffatt. He was a gifted communicator and teacher who gave me my passion for social justice, taught me how to think independently and always supported me even when he disagreed with me. His conversation, kindness, wit and wisdom are greatly missed.

What's the point of writing when I don't know how to read?

(comment during Southwark INFORM group discussions)

CONTENTS

TABLE OF FIGURES

NOTE ON TERMINOLOGY

The term "learning difficulty" is used throughout this book to describe people with mental impairments who need support to live in the community. The term replaces the old phrase "mental handicap" and is used in preference to this and "learning disability" as it is the preferred term of user groups such as People First.

Throughout the book I use the term "we" to describe people like myself who are responsible for providing or purchasing services. I use this term not to exclude people but to point out the responsibility service providers and purchasers have for making sure accessible information is available and as an acknowledgement of the immense power services still have over people's lives. I thus use "we" to remind those of us who work for people with learning difficulties that we are all responsible for this and we all have a part to play in redressing the power imbalance.

Acknowledgements

So many people were involved in the Southwark INFORM project it would be difficult to name them all individually. I would however like to thank the following without whom none of this would have been possible:

All the people who I interviewed for "The Right to Know"

All the people who told me what they thought of the tape, video and posters

The photography group who made the "Health, Home and Happiness" posters

Entelechy who made the "Check It Out!" video

Southwark Unity Self-advocacy group who were with me all the way

All the people at the Grange and Queen's Road Day Centres who were so helpful throughout the project

The management committee of Southwark INFORM

Southwark Consortium

The NDIP team at the Policy Studies Institute

The Department of Health

Southwark Social Services

People to People

Camberwell Advocacy

Only Connect

Fastforward

Garden House

Southwark Disablement Association

Keyring

ONIS

Blue River

Brook Drive

Very special thanks to: Annette Mc Donald, Jane Lewis, Gaby Mitchell, Sarah Lees, Andre Steele, Julie Lomax, Steven Rose, Jimmy Clark, Catherine Flynn, for their tremendous support throughout the work of the project, and (in some cases) their advice and comments on various stages of the text.

And finally I am indebted to Simon Duffy who acted as my supporter, adviser and mentor throughout the whole of the Southwark INFORM project.

About the author

Virginia Moffatt has been involved in the lives of people with learning difficulties since 1984, as a volunteer, paid supporter, advocate and friend. Since 1989, she has worked primarily in Southwark, as a day centre worker for Southwark Social Services, the co-ordinator of the Corali Dance Company, and Information Worker and later Project Leader of Southwark INFORM. She is currently employed by Southwark Consortium as the Individual Contracts Manager where she is committed to the development of individualised services and continues to campaign for more accessible information. She has a BSc in Biology that she never uses and an MSc in Voluntary Sector Organisation. In the unlikely event of her retirement she would like to spend the rest of her life reading and looking at mountains.

Preface

My father was an English teacher so from an early age words, language and meaning were important to me. It wasn't until I started getting to know people who had learning difficulties however, that I discovered there are more means than one to communicate. Over the years I have been challenged to find new ways to talk to people, through sound, sight, touch, signing, symbols, using tapes, photographs, pictures and other media.

From 1992 to 1994 I worked at Southwark INFORM, a voluntary organisation funded by the Department of Health, as part of the National Disability Information Project. Southwark INFORM had a brief to improve information provision for people with learning difficulties and disabled people from ethnic minority communities. This involved discovering the information needs of the target groups and exploring ways to make information more accessible. I was responsible for the work with people with learning difficulties which fell into three stages.

In the initial months of the project I interviewed users, providers and carers about the information needs of people with learning difficulties. The findings were written up and widely distributed (Moffatt, 1993a). Stage two was to transform a written information directory (Moffatt, 1993b) into three different accessible resources, an audiotape, a series of photographic posters and a video. During this time I had so many requests for help in writing documents more simply that I also produced a guide on the subject (Moffatt, 1993c). The final stage of the project was to run a series of facilitated meetings with users of services and support staff to find out what they thought of the resources. The findings of this research were produced in a report that examined the usefulness of each resource and made some recommendations about future usage (Moffatt, 1994).

This book draws together the key findings of all these reports. In doing so I have been able to revise the initial work extensively and include examples of good practice that have emerged in the last three years. During this time I have been encouraged to see people across the country becoming more aware of the need to make information accessible for all. However many of these changes have been very small and we still live in a world where jargon predominates and the written word holds sway.

Life without jargon challenges those of us who purchase or provide services to be different. It means involving people who use services in the production of information. It means taking time to help people understand. It means investing money in quality resources. It means using a variety of different ways to tell people and it always, always means keeping it simple! Life without jargon challenges us to be courageous. Informed people will have more power to demand their rights. We have to be brave enough to respond to such demands and concede power when necessary. But life without jargon also liberates us from always being in control, from always giving people what we think they want and from hiding what we really mean behind long unintelligible words. Life without jargon is exciting, fun and above all possible when we're prepared to work at it and make it happen.

If you're interested to know more about making your information accessible, this book can help you find out how. If you're really serious about doing it - the rest will be up to you.

Virginia Moffatt

London, October 1995

An accessible summary

Life Without Jargon is a book that is intended for people providing and purchasing services to help them think how to inform people with learning difficulties. As a result, it is written in complex language and is not accessible to people who use services.

However, I do feel it would be useful for people with learning difficulties if they could understand the basic message of the book. I have thus summarised the essential points in this section. I have aimed to use simple language and have used the rebus symbol system since it is still the most commonly used one today (see page 32). I am aware that this attempt is still a long way from being truly accessible, and I still struggle with ways to make complex issues easy for people to grasp. This is my best shot to date and any comments, criticisms or further suggestions will be welcomed by contacting me at Southwark Consortium, 27, Barry Road, SE22 0HX.

INTRODUCTION

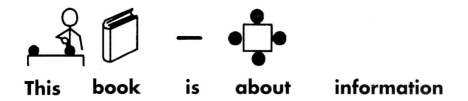

This   book   is   about   information

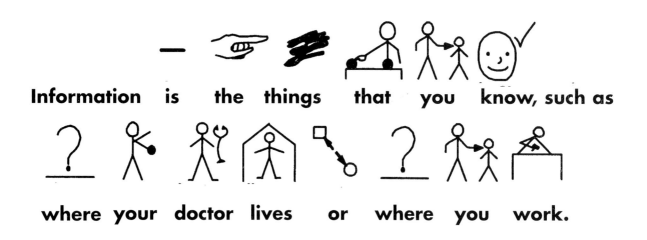

Information   is   the   things   that   you   know, such as

where your doctor lives   or   where   you   work.

When   you   do   not   know   something   you   need

to   find   out!

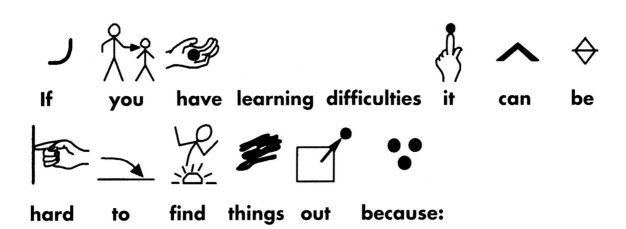

If you have learning difficulties it can be

hard to find things out because:

1. Sometimes staff tell you what to do. So

it is not easy to ask for help

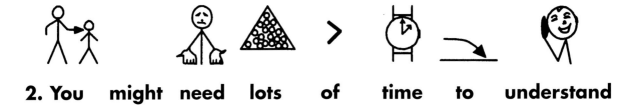

2. You might need lots of time to understand

3. Sometimes people use long words that you

can not understand.

4. People write information. This is no good

if you can not read.

THINGS YOU MIGHT WANT TO KNOW

People in Southwark told me they wanted to

know about:

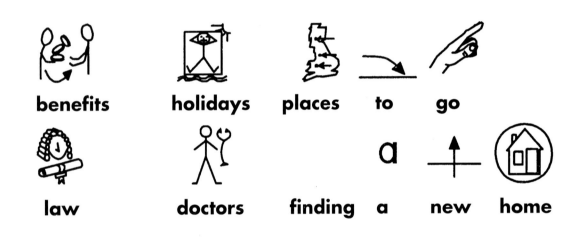

benefits   holidays   places to go

law   doctors   finding a new home

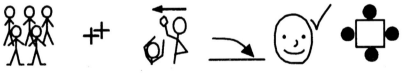

People also wanted to know about:

Love **& Sex** **Taking** **care** **of** **your** **children**

Sexual **abuse** **Staying** **well** **How** **to** **vote**

Self advocacy **Community** **Care**

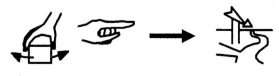

USE   THE   RIGHT   WAYS:

If   you   can   not   read   you   need   to   find

out   in   different   ways   such   as:

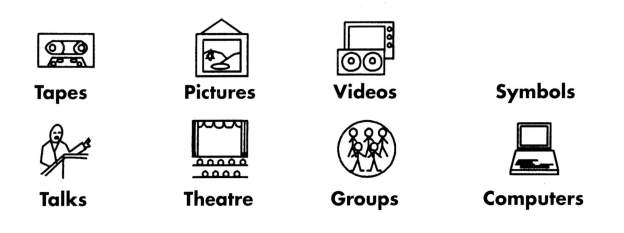

Tapes   **Pictures**   **Videos**   **Symbols**

Talks   **Theatre**   **Groups**   **Computers**

In   Southwark   we   tried   tapes,   pictures   and   videos.

People   liked   them   because

1. They   found things out

2. People   with   learning difficulties were   in   the

pictures   and   videos

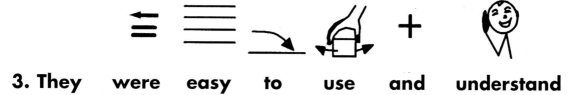

3. They   were   easy   to   use   and   understand

HOW TO HELP PEOPLE WITH LEARNING

DIFFICULTIES KNOW THINGS

1. Make it easy for people to understand

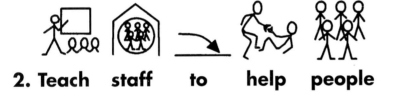

2. Teach staff to help people

3. Spend money on making tapes and videos.

4. Make sure staff have time to help.

5. Work together.

So you want people to understand you?

1 A powerless past

The recent history of people with learning difficulties in Britain has been one of institution-alisation and oppression. The Victorian belief that people with learning difficulties were "idiots" who were "uneducable" ultimately led to the development of large mental handi-cap hospitals situated in remote country locations. The initial intentions may have been benevolent, but, whatever the intentions, the result was to isolate people with learning dif-ficulties from their societies and place them in hospitals which mistreated and institution-alised them (Ryan and Thomas, 1980).

It was a common experience for people living in hospital to suffer physical and verbal abuse, be denied choices and rights, and have few educational, social or employment opportunities. Those people who lived in the community fared little better. They too had restricted choices, went to institutionalised day centres and had limited opportunities for employment and education (Ryan and Thomas, 1980; Brechin and Walmsley, 1989; Atkinson and Williams, 1990).

As a result of such experiences, the majority of people with learning difficulties have become used to services that allow them no say and render them powerless. Furthermore, negative stereotyping, reflected by labels such as "ineducable" and "subnormal" or media perceptions of people as "mad", "pathetic", "eternal children", "sad", or "sick" (Ryan and Thomas, 1980; Wertheimer, 1987), has caused many people with learning difficulties to have low self-esteem and self-confidence.

In the last twenty-five years, attempts have been made to counteract these years of repres-sion and negative labelling. The 1971 White Paper "Better Services for the Mentally Handicapped" (HMSO, 1971) led to an acknowledgement that people with learning diffi-culties should be able to live in their local communities along with their fellow citizens. This has resulted in the closure of many large hospitals, resulting in many people moving back into the areas where they were born - the much publicised Community Care Policy (Dowson, 1991). In addition the work of Wolfensburger on "normalisation" and O'Brien on "social role valorisation" assumed that people with learning difficulties should have the right to participate in their local communities, should have the same choices and opportu-nities as their fellow citizens and should be treated with dignity and respect (Brechin and Walmsley, 1989).

The most recent NHS and Community Care Act of 1990 (HMSO, 1990) has re-inforced the government's commitment to providing care in the community for people with learning difficulties. This has resulted in a speeding up of the hospital closure programme and peo-ple beginning to live in a variety of different supported arrangements with mixed results (Dowson, 1991; Duffy, 1992a,b,c; Simons, 1994; Cox and Pearson, 1995). Other key ele-ments of the act have also had an impact on people's lives. Social Services are now required to consult service users about their views as part of the community care planning processes. People living in the community are entitled to a community care assessment of need, a package of appropriate support and information about service availability (HMSO, 1990). People with learning difficulties have thus been given the right to information at a time when there is so much more to know. Having access to such information will thus be crucial in increasing the power people have in the services they receive. This is particularly important if we want to provide people with real opportunities and choices and counter the criticisms that community care just results in more abuse of people with learning diffi-culties (Cox and Pearson, 1995).

Furthermore the community care reforms have happened against a background of changes in the way we all receive information. The rise of tabloid journalism means we are far more knowledgeable about the lives of public figures than we used to be (although whether this is advantageous is a matter for some debate!). Whilst communications technology has developed dramatically, with satellite television, the internet and even video telephones creating new possibilities for the speed at which we find things out. Despite the failure of the most recent freedom of information bill (Fisher, 1993), the government has come under more pressure to make information more available to the public. The Citizen's Charter, performance tables, the public appearance of the Director of MI5 are all small signs that in some circumstances the government is making information more available. The right to information thus goes way beyond community care. If we really want people with learning difficulties to have a valued place within the community, we need to acknowledge that they are part of this wider picture too.

The old adage "knowledge is power" has never been more pertinent. But when we think about how to inform people with learning difficulties we have to recognise two factors. Firstly, their unique history in this country means that their information needs may be vastly different from that of other citizens. And secondly, as the following chapters will demonstrate, the words we use and the way the information is presented will need to be different too. In the next section we will look at some of the issues we need to consider if we truly wish to make our information accessible.

2 Current Complexities

We have seen so far that people with learning difficulties have survived in services that have made them powerless. Such powerlessness can be, in part, addressed by enabling people to receive information. However, before we do so we need to be aware of the effects of disempowerment, the different ways people understand information and the context in which they live.

The effect of disempowerment

Imagine living in a ward for thirty years where every decision is made for you by your staff team, where tea is always served at the same time (and you never have the choice of coffee), and where if you ever ask for something different you get into trouble. Or imagine going to school and being told every day that you are stupid, growing up in an area where people called you names like "spas" and "mongol" and spending the next twenty years of your life in a day centre where you do the same old thing year in, year out.

Imagine your life suddenly changing, leaving hospital to live in an ordinary house in the street, or having the opportunity to go to adult education classes or try out a job. It is likely that you will experience overwhelming emotions. Your new life may be exciting, but it is also likely to be terrifying and confusing. You will be presented with lots of things you never even dreamed of, all at once: choosing coffee instead of tea, going to the shops, filling in job applications. Things that the rest of us take for granted will seem intimidating and frightening tasks. If asking for things has got you into trouble in the past, you will probably find it difficult to say what you want. And if you've never had a choice before, you will need a great deal of support to understand the significance of different options.

The experiences described above are common to people with learning difficulties (Brechin and Walmsley, 1989; Ryan and Thomas, 1980). Practically every person I have ever worked with has told me similar stories, or I have witnessed them having similar experiences. Even in supposedly enlightened community care settings, I have often seen situations where supporters control, intimidate and restrict choices, and where service users are almost too frightened to breathe.

Before we can begin to inform people with learning difficulties we need to recognise the incredible amount of power we hold in every encounter we have. We also need to recognise that people are going to need an awful lot of time to learn to trust us so that they can tell us what they want in their lives and what they need to know to get it. Good support to people with learning difficulties means looking for as many ways to give power back to people as possible, whether it be simply giving a choice of drink, or enabling someone to disagree with us.

Finally, we need to provide places where people with learning difficulties feel safe and secure to talk about their wants, needs and desires without the worry that they will suffer for expressing them. User groups are immensely powerful, particularly where they offer people the opportunity to talk about their deepest feelings. This is clearly demonstrated by the experience of black user groups, men's groups, women's groups, relationship and sexuality groups that are run across South London by a variety of different organisations (see Resources list for details). The self-advocacy movement has also demonstrated that self-advocacy groups can enable people to come together to talk about common areas of oppression and gain a collective voice to challenge services. If we provide such places we will give people the confidence to ask for information and to demand accessible information.

People are different

Everybody, whether they have a learning difficulty or not, has a different capacity for absorbing and retaining information. Whilst some people with learning difficulties will be able to understand information relatively quickly, others may have severe communication difficulties and multiple disablties which limit their understanding.

A variety of methods for making information accessible will thus have to be developed in order to ensure individuals can choose the most appropriate form from them. It is also important to recognise that people will require different levels of information. Someone with low support needs, living fairly independently will want to know where she or he can claim benefits, how to organise a holiday or move house. However, an individual with complex support needs or multiple disabilities may simply want to know if she or he is going out today.

The complexity of service provision

Figure 1 illustrates the complexity of services available to people with learning difficulties. As we can see, one individual may be in receipt of services from several different organisations, be they Social Services, Health Services, Voluntary Agencies, Housing, or Leisure and Recreation. Conversely, it is also likely that some people receive very few of these services or none at all. The overall picture is of a tattered spider's web, with different agencies connecting with each other through one or more threads of varying strength, or in some instances having no links at all.

Furthermore, the picture is rarely (if ever!) static. Large bureaucratic structures reorganise, agencies move, services lose their funding, staff leave. Service providers thus need an awareness of each other's services and have the responsibility to communicate effectively with service users and carers.

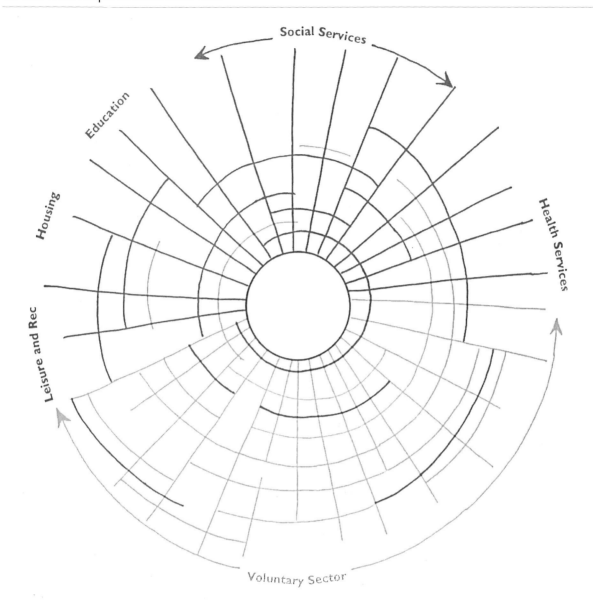

Figure 1 The web of services

Although this picture describes Southwark services it is probably not that dissimilar to other areas. Wherever people with learning difficulties live in the community there will be a variety of organisations working with them in many different ways. The market that has been created by the onset of community care also means that, in all likelihood, there will be an expansion of different support providers in every area as new organisations are set up. The web if anything is likely to become more complicated over time.

Carers and service providers need information too

If carers and service providers are to support people with learning difficulties properly, they will also have information needs. Having a good understanding of what's available will be of use in educating service users about their rights, advocating on their behalf and ensuring they can participate fully in their local community.

Services are bureaucratic

The ideal service model would be the service user having an equal partnership with the service provider as in Figure 2.

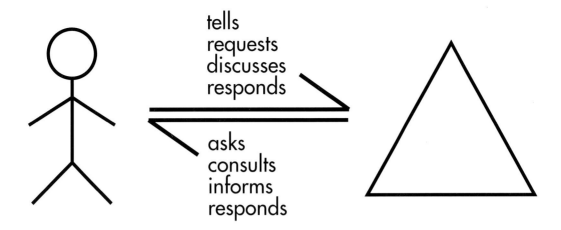

Figure 2 A partnership

Unfortunately, the reality is closer to Figure 3, with service users being at the bottom of a huge hierarchical chain. It is the nature of bureaucracy for information to be sifted out at every level, whether intentionally or not (Handy, 1985).

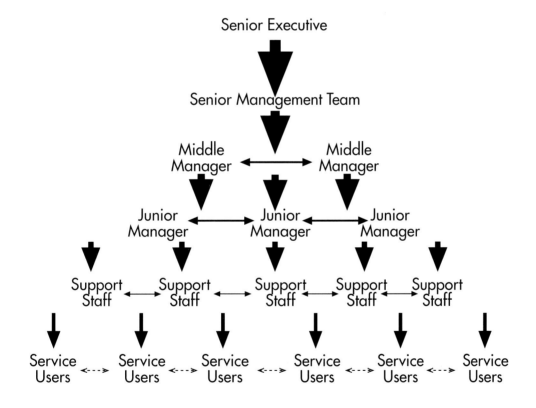

Figure 3 The bureaucratic relationship

Services thus need to understand that at every level they have a responsibility for ensuring information is freely available both to service users, support workers, managers and between departments.

Working in isolation gets us nowhere

We all have a part to play in the giving and receiving of information. We thus have a responsibility to ensure that we talk to each other. If we are not keeping each other well informed, it is highly unlikely that we will be informing people using services!

So what do you want to know?

Defining the information needs of people with learning difficulties

The Southwark Inform Consultancy identified two broad areas of information need. One area is around the availability of services, whilst the second is around broader social issues. Whilst some of these needs may have been specific to Southwark it is likely that they are of more general significance, and indeed other information projects have highlighted this (O'Farrell, 1993).

1   Services: Where do I go for that?

The first kind of information need was around people's rights, services and local and national activities. The list that has arisen out of these is by no means comprehensive, as people's information needs will change with changing services, topical issues and life circumstances. It includes:

- benefits
- accessible venues
- respite care
- leisure, social or community activities
- legal issues/rights
- statutory responsibilities of local or national government
- statementing
- finding a GP with a positive attitude
- services for elderly people with learning difficulties
- grant aid for individuals and projects
- holidays
- equipment
- bus passes, taxicards and transport
- making wills or trust funds
- tracing people who have left large hospitals
- housing
- integrated services
- funding for staff to go on holiday with people

With so many people moving back into the community, it is not surprising that information on benefits and leisure activities emerged as the most common themes. Nor is it surprising that the other very common need was for information on holidays. Service users are becoming more aware that they do have choices where they could go, and there is always a need for parents and carers to know of supported holidays that would provide them with some respite.

This type of information need can be met fairly easily through a resource directory or specific information agency. It may involve giving out a telephone number or advising on a course of action. However there are some issues that arise out of trying to meet this need.

What if a service is not available?

The current climate of cuts in public expenditure means that sometimes services are not available. For example during the consultancy it emerged that in some social service homes there was little available in terms of financing support staff to accompany people on holiday. Every year it seems that a community group is cut and fewer and fewer people receive day services. It can feel very negative to be saying a service does not exist.

However, there is a role for an independent information agency to tell people what they are entitled to. This means that people will be better informed and will thus be able to advocate for themselves. Better informed people will also create a pressure for better services as purchasers and providers will be unable to claim there is no demand for a service that people are shouting about!

Changing information, duplication, gaps in services

This is a feature of all information provision and is not unique to information for people with learning difficulties. Resource directories are useful, but they quickly become outdated, whilst different organisations might produce directories to different time scales containing slightly different information.

Given the complexity of services illustrated in Figure 1, it is not surprising that each service might be unaware of what the other provides. For example, one residential support provider was unaware of a specialist adult education site half a mile down the road. It is also unsurprising that small voluntary projects will find it difficult to get their information to larger organisations. One lady who worked a 7 hour week found it almost impossible to publicise her work because she was unable to attend staff meetings to tell services about it and her written information was often lost in the system.

Regular information forums may be one way of bringing services together to share knowledge and work that's happening. Service providers also need to be aware that they need to be pro-active in telling service users, carers and information agencies about their services. If information directories are produced there needs to be a commitment to updating them regularly. It is possible that an area wide database, that could be accessed by a lot of agencies, could be a way of partly overcoming this problem.

Staff turnover

Staff turnover can be quite high in day and residential support services. New staff entering an area may have little awareness of what's going on there. Whilst they are learning, others are leaving taking valuable knowledge with them. Services need to consider how to inform staff of relevant agencies in the area so that new staff do not constantly reinvent the wheel.

Induction programmes should always involve orientation in the locality. Services could also encourage staff to collect information to be held in one place creating a local information resource that could be accessible for service users (see p.40). Services could also think of ways to bring staff from all levels together through joint training, working parties and so on.

2   Broader information issues

As a result of the institutionalisation and lack of social and educational opportunities described earlier, many people with learning difficulties have missed out on years of knowledge that their fellow citizens might take for granted.

It is important that such broader areas are addressed because they affect very personal elements of people's lives. If we as providers are to ensure that people are able to make real choices, we also need to ensure that they are given the right information and enough time to absorb and understand it.

Sexuality

As described earlier, people with learning difficulties have been stereotyped negatively and are often considered to be either asexual "eternal children" or promiscous sexual animals (Wertheimer, 1987). The result is that many people are confused by their sexual feelings which may lead them to act inappropriately, for example by masturbating or exposing themselves in public. This can lead to punitive action, which leads to more confusion and loss of self-esteem. It is also common for people to be prevented from clearly expressing their sexual feelings for another person, because parents and carers are frightened of where the relationship might lead. Finally, lack of education and institutionalisation can lead to low self-esteem and low body awareness, which makes people especially vulnerable to abuse.

There is clearly a need for good sex education which is being slowly recognised, and many resources have come to light in recent years. These include Ann Craft's "Living Your Life" pack (Craft, 1992) and videos such as "Release Me" (Lea, 1993) and "My Choice, My Own Choice" (Health First!, 1992).

There is also a need for service providers to support service users in learning about sex in situations that are safe and non-threatening. This raises many issues for services:

- Staff need to be very skilled and confident in providing information about sexuality. This requires a commitment to offering regular training and clear policies for people to work with.

- Staff need to treat each situation with sensitivity and consideration of each individual's needs. This means recognising that some people may want a sexual relationship whilst others may not; religious beliefs may be a factor in developing a sexual relationship; it may not be appropriate to explore sexuality with every individual.

- Staff need to be non-judgemental of people's sexual orientation.

- Many parents and carers will be understandably concerned about the idea of their relative developing a sexual relationship. Staff need to respect these concerns and work with parents and carers to enable them to feel confident about any relationship their relative may be involved in.

- Sex education should also include information about HIV/AIDS and other sexual diseases.

Parenting

Just as sexual issues have taken a long time to emerge, so have issues around parenting. In the last three years this has become more pertinent in Southwark and nationally. Several individuals in Southwark have either become parents or been identified to services as needing support to be parents.

Here too people require a huge amount of information, around pregnancy, the process of childbirth, and ongoing support for rearing children. Having a child is a huge responsibility for all of us, whether we have a disability or not. Many people with learning difficulties may have had fewer experiences of watching people parent and may have a false picture of what it means to have a child. The reality of the sleepless nights, changing nappies, feeding and protecting their children will be a huge adjustment and moreso without adequate information, preparation and support.

"Parentability" a support group for parents with disabilities and the National Childbirth Trust has begun to look at developing resources for people with learning difficulties (Parentability, 1993). Whilst the Special Parenting Service in Cornwall has been pioneering specialist support services for several years and now have a video of their work (Special Parenting Service, 1993).

Sexual abuse

Sexual abuse is frighteningly high in services for people with learning difficulties and too often goes undetected (Brown, 1992). If services are to respond to this they need to ensure the following:

- Good operational policies and reporting procedures need to be in place so that staff feel confident there is a process for detecting abuse and dealing with it. This should also deter potential abusers as it will send a clear signal to them that abuse is not to be tolerated.

- Disclosure of sexual abuse requires a high level of trust from the victim, and a confident response from the person who hears it. Often the first person to hear a disclosure of sexual abuse is a member of staff who has little or no experience of abuse. Staff thus need training in the necessary skills if they are to respond appropriately.

- Sexual abuse is extremely frightening and distressing for the victim, for staff supporting them and for families and friends. When it is revealed services need to ensure that everyone involved has ready and easy access to counselling if they need it and are given as much time as they need to talk about it.

- Sexual abuse in a service is a huge betrayal of trust to the victim and their families and friends. It is often tempting for a service to be secretive about the disclosure of abuse because it does not wish to admit that it has committed such a betrayal of trust. Since abuse relies on secrecy the best weapon to fight it with is openness and honesty with people when it happens. Whilst the victim and their supporters will rightly be angry and upset about what has happened, they will be much more appreciative of a service that admits responsibility, tries to find out what went wrong, and to ensure it does not happen again, than one that does not.

Several organisations also now campaign for or provide support to survivors of sexual abuse, such as VOICE in Derbyshire, RESPOND and Beverley Lewis House in London.

Health

The living conditions in hospital were often quite poor (Ryan and Thomas, 1980) so many people left them in a state of poor health and with little awareness of how to look after themselves. Furthermore the great emphasis on social care over the last 15 years has meant that services have not always had a great awareness of people's health needs. The following lists indicates some of the relevant issues.

- Many people have weight problems due to a lack of awareness about the importance of taking exercise and eating healthily. Weight problems can also be symptoms of low self esteem and unhappiness. Thus people need to have opportunities to learn about diet and exercise and to be supported to talk about problems they might have with eating.

- Smoking is very common in institutions like hospitals and day centres. It is likely that people are not always aware of the risks associated with smoking or how to give it up if they wish to.

- Services need to be aware that Hepatitis B was prevalent in many institutions, and as a result there may be a high incidence of carriers among people with learning difficulties. Service users and staff all need to know the implications of this and preventative action they can take if they wish.

- Many service users are on drugs to control aspects of their behaviours or mental health problems. Service users often have little control over these drugs or knowledge of their side effects. This is also of concern to carers and support staff who may lack adequate knowledge to support the service user.

Health has become higher on the national agenda with the publication of "Health of the Nation" (Department of Health, 1992) and this has had an impact on strategies for people with learning difficulties (Department of Health, 1995). A recent study of the health information needs of people with learning difficulties highlighted that most people's information needs were very individual and would need to be provided in appropriate formats (Greenhalgh, 1994). Whilst work in Bolton has demonstrated the success of looking at the whole person's health needs (McMillan, 1995). Southwark Consortium is hoping to replicate this project in Southwark through the recent appointment of a specialist nurse to work with people about their health needs.

Politics

Politics is a complicated business and people need to be aware of how to vote, what the different parties are saying and who the different candidates are.

Such information has to be presented in a factual unbiased form. It is all too easy to influence service users by having strong opinions about the relative merits of the different parties. Sometimes it might be more appropriate to bring an outsider in to relieve support staff from this difficulty, though this is not without problems. I was unable to do a presentation at a day centre during the 1992 election because it was viewed as canvassing on council property, which is against council regulations.

Bereavement

It is all too common for people with learning difficulties to have experienced a major bereavement without being adequately informed. Many service providers and carers have mistakenly believed that a person with a learning difficulty will be best protected if they do not know that a friend or relative has died. Such assumptions are misguided as people will always know something is wrong if their friend or relative stops visiting. If they are not told why, it is possible that they will assume the person has left them or they have done something to upset them (Oswin, 1992).

Services need to ensure the following:

- Training and support needs to be provided for staff to enable them to assist people who are grieving.

- Clear guidelines should be in place to help staff know how to react in times of bereavement.

- Staff need to talk to service users about what's happened, explaining relevant traditions, so that the person can choose whether she or he wishes to attend the funeral or not.

- Staff need to ensure that anniversaries and birthdays are remembered and that the bereaved person is encouraged to talk about their loss.

- Staff need to let people know where their friend or relative is buried or cremated, so they can visit if they want to.

- A major bereavement can be an extremely emotional event for the individual and staff supporting them. Services need to ensure both staff and users have access to counselling in times of bereavement if they want it.

Personal Safety

It was stated earlier that many people with learning difficulties have moved into their local communities fairly recently. Many people may be unaware of the risks involved in talking to strangers, opening the door late at night, not entering into confrontational situations with strangers and so on.

Services need to prepare people by giving guidance about these areas regularly and by having a good back-up system so people know where to call for help.

Race awareness and cultural identity

If people have been isolated from their communities, they may be unaware of the rights and needs of people of different races. Such ignorance can lead to unintentional racism and it is important that services address this issue in a positive and supportive way.

- Staff should always behave in a non-racist fashion.

- Staff should challenge racist comments and explain to users in a supportive way why they are not acceptable.

- Staff should provide users with opportunities to learn about each other's cultures and encourage users to tell each other about their different cultural traditions.

- Services should appoint staff of the same culture and who speak the same language as the individual.

- Services should ensure people's personal care, food, lifestyle, community and family contact reflect their family background

Despite the influential report *Double Discrimination* about these issues, (Baxter et al, 1990), services have been slow to pick up on them. The recent book, *Give us a Voice* shows that it is still difficult for people from ethnic minorities to have access to their local communities, traditions, cultural foods and religions (Lewis, 1996). Organisations need to learn from both these books and apply their recommendations if they are to offer culturally appropriate services.

Community Care

The 1990 NHS and Community Care Act referred to earlier, obliges services to provide users with information on service availability, to consult service users about the community care plans and to provide a procedure for people to complain about services.

All of these elements involve a vast array of information and a multitude of agencies described by confusing acronyms such as JCCPG (Joint Community Care Planning Group) and LSLHC (Lambeth, Southwark and Lewisham Health Commission). The relevant documents are usually over wordy, full of jargon, written in small print and are off-putting to most users and carers regardless of reading ability.

It is very easy to do consultation badly! Good consultation requires the following:

- Information needs to be provided in accessible formats (see page 27). Written documents should be expressed in clear and simple language that is easy to understand.

- Information about different things needs to be provided at different times. Too much information at once is confusing and unhelpful.

- The best way to find out what people think about services is to meet them on their own terms by going to user groups regularly to talk and listen to people's opinions.

- Consultation needs to be seen as an ongoing process, rather than an annual token exercise.

- Consultation meetings that are followed by cuts programmes will do nothing to increase the level of trust between users and providers. It is important therefore to give people a true picture of the finances and try and work together to use them in the best way.

- People will become rapidly disillusioned with taking part in consultation exercises if nothing ever changes. Good consultation should thus result in action!

Another important aspect of community care is the right of the individual to have an assessment of need. People need to have this information, know they have a right to an advocate and understand what this information means for them. Such information needs to be presented accessibly and people need time to understand this complicated process (People First, 1992).

Self-advocacy

It is also important to note that information and self-advocacy will always be closely linked. As self-advocacy groups have grown stronger in the last few years, the challenge to services to provide information in more appropriate formats has also strengthened. People First have started a "Make it Easy" project which continues to keep the issues alive nationally; whilst local self-advocacy projects such as Southwark Unity, Lewisham Voice, Lambeth People First, Advocacy in Gateshead, Avon People First and many more have been involved in accessible information projects and will undoubtedly continue to be so.

The next step

The list is not a comprehensive one but it indicates the wide range of issues that people with learning difficulties need to know about. Such information is very complicated to pass on as it encompasses a whole range of social and educational needs. In order to ensure people are adequately informed on these issues services should recognise that long term strategies and a variety of methods will be needed.

The constant theme running through this is: knowing what the need is not enough. If we really want to inform people we need to do so with jargon free words and in ways that go beyond the written word. In the next chapter we will explore some of the ways we can make information more accessible.

Beyond the written word

How to make information accessible

1   What's the point of writing when I don't know how to read?

A colleague just came into the office with a huge pile of papers in his hand. He was bemoaning the fact that they had only arrived on his desk in the previous two days and that in all likelihood they would be incomprehensible and stuffed full of jargon. My colleague and I are both literate and adept with written language yet all too often we find ourselves puzzling over what such documents mean. If it's difficult for us to understand jargon, how much more difficult must it be for people who use our services! The majority of people with learning difficulties cannot read, write or understand long words, whether through lack of decent education or the nature of their disability. Yet we still persist in producing all our information in written documents that are completely meaningless to them.

Our society places a great deal of emphasis on the value of the written word despite the fact that many people (and not just people with learning difficulties) have difficulties reading and writing. When the people who have information (usually purchasers or providers of services) present it in a way that people with learning difficulties don't understand, the information providers remain powerful and controlling. If those of us purchasing or providing services wish to change this status quo we need to change our mindsets. We need to answer the question that was recently posed to me "What's the point of writing when I don't know how to read?" and think afresh about the way we inform and the words we use.

Whilst I was working at Southwark INFORM, in a sense I learnt nothing new. People with learning difficulties had been saying for a long time that they needed information presented in alternative ways (West, unpublished 1992; Rowlands, unpublished, 1992). However the project did provide me with the opportunity to bring these ideas together and give them more publicity (Moffatt, 1993a; Moffatt, 1993c). Furthermore it provided me with the opportunity to produce some accessible information resources and find out what people thought of them (Moffatt, 1994).

In this chapter I will present a range of possible ways to inform people with learning difficulties. Some were formally evaluated by the work of Southwark INFORM, whilst some were tried out without formal evaluation. Others have been tried by people in different parts of the country. Finally there are other ideas that you may want to try for yourself. The essential message for you to take away from this chapter is that there are many ways to tell people and different people will want to find out in different ways. The methods described here will work best when you are involving people with learning difficulties in the process, using language they understand and finding out which methods they would prefer.

2   The Southwark INFORM Directory - Making it Easy

I outlined some of the information needs of people with learning difficulties above and stated that some of this information could be provided relatively easily through a directory. One of the earliest pieces of work I undertook at the project was to produce a written directory of local services (Moffatt, 1993b). The directory was intended in the first instance to be something that could be of use to staff working in services. Although the language was intentionally kept simple, and the directory was illustrated, it was never intended as a fully accessible document for people using services. Instead it acted as a starting point for creating three accessible resources, an audiotape, a series of posters and a video. All three resources were distributed across all the services in Southwark and piloted through a series of facilitated meetings with service users and supporters (Moffatt, 1994) for further details on methodology please contact the author direct.

In this section I will look at each of these three resources in turn, how they were produced, the content and what people thought of them.

3 Audiotape - "The I Want to Know" tape

The tape was produced from my text by the Gateshead AIRS project. It contained all the information in the written directory, except that relating to carers. The tape was 60 minutes in length.

I felt it was important that the tape was easy to listen to so that people could concentrate on what it was telling them. I thus made sure the language was as simple as possible and the information was divided into sections. I asked Gateshead AIRS to separate each section with music and sound effects. They also used several different voices that helped break up the text.

I chose Gateshead AIRS because they were cheaper than many of the other taping organisations, had a library of sound effects and had worked with self-advocacy groups in Gateshead. They produced 200 tapes for us at a cost of £660, £3.30 per tape.

The majority of people coming to the meetings liked the tape for several reasons:

Accessibility

"It is her only way of getting independent information"

The tape was immensely accessible. The language was clear and easy to follow, and the use of sound effects, music, different headings and different voices made it easy to listen to. It was good to listen to it as a group, which provided opportunities for people to go back over things they had not understood and to re-wind and listen to it again. It was best when played in sections and some people enjoyed putting it in the machines. The tape was particularly good for people who could not read but could understand spoken language including people with visual impairments.

Knowledge

"It told me something interesting"

Many people responded positively to the contents of the tape. They felt it gave them ideas about things to do and was very informative about things that were available locally. People felt that they had learnt things they did not know before.

Status

The tape told people about things they thought were important such as sexuality, employment, drama. It also talked about places people were familiar with like their day centres, projects they used, schools they had been to. The fact that this information was presented in a way that was accessible gave status to things that people thought were important.

Privacy

The tape could be listened to in private at home or on a Walkman. This gave people some control over the information they received and the power to ask for help when they needed it.

Limitations

The tape did have some limitations. Some of these were due to design factors: there was no inlay card, the items were in a different order from the written directory, there was too much information and some of the information was incorrect. All these things made it difficult for people to follow where they were on the tape.

These problems could have been overcome. An inlay card could have been inserted detailing contents in the same order as the directory and informing you of how long each section was, making it easier for people to find their way around. The tape could have been made into several tapes, each no more than twenty minutes long, on different topics and produced in languages other than English, according to need.

A more important drawback was that the tape did not help people with limited concentration spans or hearing impairments. However, on the whole good tapes produced well will be extremely useful ways to inform people.

4   Photographs - The "Health", "Home" and "Happiness" posters

When Southwark INFORM moved to the Beormund Centre in November 1992, we were delighted to make contact with the Blackfriars Photography Project who were also based at the centre. Discussions with workers at the project led to the idea of a course for people with learning difficulties to design posters with information displayed in photographs.

I thus commissioned Blackfriars to run a fifteen week course for eight people with learning difficulties. The brief was to produce two posters on local health and social services. The group, however, had other ideas! They decided to create three posters on the themes that were important to them: health, home and happiness.

The group met from July to November 1993, completing the posters in November 1993. Each poster consisted of a picture of one of the group members representing the theme, surrounded by photographs of local services, with the name and telephone number underneath. Thus the "Health" poster was represented by Janette Charlton, dressed as a doctor, the "Home" poster by Jimmy Clark as the head of Southwark Consortium and the "Happiness" poster by Philip McGonigle, holding some flowers (because he was a keen gardener). The group themselves chose the images and the information that should go on the poster. Since they had a lot of fun on the project, the pictures are deliberately humorous and all three people look extremely happy!

The tutor for the project, Melanie Jackson, felt that the people who participated in the course gained a lot from the experience. It was good to find out about different things in the borough and about the different lives of the people in the group. It helped having time to think about the wider issues, such as getting the right help with your health, or getting the home you wanted. This served to emphasise the importance of creating information in ways that suit people. People were proud of the finished product and the fact that they were represented on the posters in images they had chosen. Sadly the group encountered hostility and discrimination in some places that made some of their visits less pleasant. The majority of places the group went to were extremely welcoming however and the project was an enjoyable experience

As with the audiotape the posters were extremely useful sources of information.

Accessibility

"I'd like to put it up for others to see"

The posters were well made and good to look at. They were easy to understand and use as a quick reference. The symbols and phone numbers were very helpful and could be used by people who could not read.

Knowledge

"They have been helpful in telling me about places I don't know about"

The posters told people new things in an interesting way. It was good that the information was limited and the little pictures round the side were excellent, as people could see the places referred to. Having a recognisable theme helped people understand what each poster was about and what they could learn from it. The posters could also be used for quick reference as people could see a picture and make the phone call.

Positive Images

"I'd like to be in the pictures!"

"He's dressed nice, he's got a tie!"

The central images were eye-catching and amusing, showing people with learning difficulties who looked good and were proud of themselves. Many people enjoyed seeing their friends and places they knew on the posters. Again this seems to have raised the status of the information as it gave a message that they were important. Since the posters could be displayed anywhere they also gave a positive message about people with learning difficulties to the wider public.

Privacy

The posters could be kept at home again giving people the choice to ask for help if they needed to.

Limitations

The posters did have some problems as some photographs were too dark; some did not clearly show what the organisation did; the "Health" poster could have had more information and been a bit clearer in the way it was presented; some information was wrong. All of these problems could be overcome by better quality and more appropriate photographs and a clearer layout. One group really felt that the "Happiness" poster misrepresented people with learning difficulties. However, since the image was selected by people with learning difficulties, we must put that one down to a matter of personal taste!

Another criticism of the posters that could be easily addressed is their lack of inclusion of people from black or ethnic minority communities. Whilst this was due to chance (all the people in the group were white), future work should always include positive images of people from these communities. The information presented should also be culturally appropriate, showing examples of local community groups.

The main limitation of posters is that that they are unhelpful for people with poor eyesight or those who find it difficult to recognise pictures.

The posters cost £4,000 to produce, and a further £400 was spent providing transport. A thousand posters of each theme were produced, thus the price for a set of three was £4.40.

Photographs could also be used in a variety of other ways such as personal albums of significant places or portable cards (see Appendix - Keep it Simple!)

5   Videotape - Check it Out!

The "Check it Out!" video was produced by a local video and drama project for people with learning difficulties, Entelechy (formerly "New Moves"). Since it is not easy to get a lot of different projects on video, I asked Entelechy to produce a 20 minute video looking at one subject - leisure in Southwark. Filming took place in January and February 1994 and the video was produced in April 1994.

The video looks at 4 local projects: a drama group, a social and counselling group, a sports project, a dance company; and 2 local places of interest: Tower Bridge and the Lavender Pump House. The video is presented by a young man with learning difficulties who visits each place and shows what goes on there. Each section is separated by music and the names and addresses appear at the end of each visit. The video also uses a signer at the end of each section, who briefly explains what happens at each project. As with the posters, the video is intentionally humorous and is presented in a lively fashion.

Two hundred videos were produced at a cost of £5,000. This made a price of £25.00 per video. This was significantly more expensive than the audiotape and posters, and this price is a reflection of the level of quality of the production. The video could have been produced more cheaply elsewhere, but the quality would have been significantly reduced.

All three resources were advertised and distributed widely in Southwark; through the launch events and through the different services. Fewer videos were distributed as many people did not actually have video machines.

Accessibility

"I watched it twice it was so good!"

The video was good entertainment and gave people the chance to really see what happened in a place. It was thus easy to follow. Having a signer helped deaf people understand what was going on. People could rewind it and go over bits they didn't understand. It was well made and good to look at.

Knowledge

"I didn't know you could go inside Tower Bridge!"

"I liked the drama, didn't know about that"

As with the other resources, the video told people about places they had not heard of in a way that was interesting.

Positive Images

"The man's got a smart shirt and a mike, he looks good"

"Smashing because there were lots of people we knew"

As with the posters, the use of a presenter with learning difficulties helped give people a sense of pride in themselves. Seeing people and places they knew also raised the status of the information. This video could also be used to present positive images to the wider public.

Privacy

Where people had videos, they could use them at home, again giving them more control.

Limitations

This particular video did suffer from some limitations. The signing was a bit confusing and the credits and other writing should have been read out. These limitations could have been overcome by having a signer present throughout and a voice over.

As with the other resources, more thought could have been given to involving people from ethnic minority communities in the presentation, showing information that was relevant to them and making the video available in community languages.

The main drawback to producing high quality videos is the expense. There is also a limit to the amount of information you can present on one video. These factors should be borne in mind when producing them.

Videos have also been used very successfully as ways of tackling some of the broader information issues. For example videos have been made about sexuality (Health First! 1992; Lea, 1992), complaints, (Entelechy, 1994, Lawnmowers, 1993) and parenting (Special Needs Parenting Service, 1994). The Video project at the Mental Health Media Project has also found that user groups all over the country are making videos about themselves and the things they find important.

6 Other ways to make it easy

Written symbols

Symbols are extremely helpful when trying to keep written text simple, and make it accessible to people who cannot read or write. However choosing the right system is not an easy task as the ideal symbol system does not exist at present.

Furthermore, there is an ideological debate raging about whether to use standardised systems such as rebus, makaton, or bliss which have been created by professionals or to use systems that have been developed by service users. Whilst the former could be viewed as disempowering the latter could lack coherence. I suspect that this is a debate that we will continue to have for some time to come and my dream of a universal symbolic language is a long way off.

However, everyone has to start somewhere and whatever symbol system you use, you must ensure that service users and staff have adequate training in usage and possible benefits. In Southwark we have chosen to focus on rebus following the successful "total communication" project in Somerset. This project trained support staff and service users in the use of rebus and encouraged the development of local symbols that were fed back to a central group and standardised. Further information about work in Somerset and the use of symbols and pictures in making your documents more accessible can be found in the Appendix.

Presentations

Presentations are particularly useful when informing people of some of the broader issues discussed above. Flip charts, pictures, photographs, symbols and participative games can all be used to get different ideas across. Spoken information is kept as simple as possible in language that is easy to follow. Information can be repeated and people attending can be encouraged to ask questions and say what they have learnt. Such presentations can be on a single issue or can follow a series of issues over time.

An important consideration in this process is that it will be facilitated if support staff are involved. For example, a presentation on the 1992 election held at a group home, worked well because of the staff involvement. The presentation used coloured charts to indicate the different parties, photographs of the leaders and pictures of what the different parties said they would do. At the end of this presentation the material was left in the office at the house, with a request that support staff follow the work of the presentation up. During the week before the election, service users came into the office regularly and asked questions about the pictures which the support staff were able to answer.

Support staff felt the process enabled them to pass on information without expressing their opinion as they could answer basic factual questions. And when it came to the election, there was a 100% turnout for voting and people could talk more confidently about the different parties.

Drama Projects

Drama Projects can be used to tackle some of the more complex issues and could run in conjunction with group work and teaching packs.

In the last two years, two of the foremost learning difficulty theatre groups have tackled some complex information issues through powerful drama and workshops. The Lawnmowers' "The Big Sex Show" looks at relationships and safe sex, whilst Strathcona Theatre Company's "Pain Without, Power Within: Faith Healing" explores bereavement, leaving home and sexual relationships in the context of a debate around faith healing of people with disabilities. Both productions were able to raise the issues in ways that were accessible and meaningful.

Group Work

Group work is probably an ideal medium for tackling some of the broader, more complicated, information needs described in the previous chapter. It allows issues to be discussed over the long-term enabling people to come back to things they have not understood and other accessible resources can be used at the same time. These were the reported strengths of the group work on health information undertaken by Lois Greenhalgh in Milton Keynes (Greenhalgh, 1994).

Group work was used in Southwark to explore what information itself meant. Beginning with "What do I know?" the group went on to look at "What don't I know?" before asking "How do I find out?". The Friday users' group run by the Oldham Disability Alliance (another pilot project for NDIP) used similar ideas to explore the same issue. They followed this further by using self-created symbols such as a question mark for information and "finding things out" games to help users understand the process.

Another Southwark group, the Fastforward "Pathfinders" group also helped people to find things out. Each week the group chose a place in Southwark they would like to visit. Each visit was recorded on a huge map of the borough with a picture of the place visited and the numbers of the buses they had to take to get there. This was a simple way of showing people they were finding things out and reminding them of what they had learnt afterwards.

Computing and information technology

Many day centres and adult education places have computing equipment that could easily have software installed that could provide information in pictorial language or simple words. Augmentative communication aids, such as Possum computers could also be used as ways of providing information.

New multi-media technology that has emerged in recent years, such as CD-rom that can be used with computers and CD-i that can be used with televisions, is also likely to have great application for the future. Both media are simple to follow and can provide information at a glance in a variety of formats. Though they are extremely expensive at present, it is likely that over time costs will come down and that they could be of great use in both private and public venues. Another NDIP project, the Gateshead Disability Information Project continues to develop information CD-i's (see Resources list).

7 Sensory communications

Many people with learning difficulties also have multiple disabilities. When someone has a learning difficulty, a severe physical disability, a visual impairment, a hearing impairment and no speech, it is difficult to imagine how on earth we can communicate information to them. Furthermore it is difficult to know what level to pitch any communication, because sometimes we do not know how much that person might understand.

Although Southwark INFORM did not begin to touch on the needs of this particular group of people, I did encounter agencies that were doing invaluable work in this area. SENSE, CHANGE and the RNIB have demonstrated the importance of developing appropriate environments that recognise how the impairment can affect an individual's ability to understand the world around them. These groups and others such as PLANET, Snoozelan and Gaby Mitchell of INTEGRATE in Southwark have also shown the importance of using lights, sounds, smells, colours and touch to communicate with people. A particularly imaginative use of smell was shown by the residential boarding school who used a different smelling soap for each day of the week to inform the students what the day was (details of groups working in this area are given in the Resources list).

8 Facilitated Communication

Facilitated Communication is a method of physically supporting individuals with weak muscle control or poor concentration to communicate. Whilst it is a method to help people with learning difficulties communicate information to people supporting them, rather than the other way around, I include it because it is interesting and to some extent controversial.

This way of communicating involves an individual having a facilitator who holds their arm to enable them to type their message. The way the facilitator holds the person's arm is crucial, as their role is to offer support to the individual who is given the strength to push against them and touch the keys.

This method of communicating was first discovered by Rosemary Crossley and Anne McDonald in Australia in the 1970's. Their extremely moving and dramatic story is told in their book "Annie's Coming Out" (Crossley and McDonald). It has also spread to America and Europe and is still the subject of furious debate today.

It's supporters argue that it is one way of enabling certain people to have their voices heard and can be used and taught by speech therapists, physiotherapists, support workers and families. Crucial to good communication is the relationship between the facilitator and the individual, and whilst in theory anybody can do it, the best results are achieved when the individual is supported in a familiar environment and with someone they trust. It's detractors argue that it is too easy for the facilitator to control the action of the person's arm and hence the communication, scientific studies do not validate it and that the results apparently achieved are unrealistic.

Although each side can produce stacks of evidence to back up their arguments, it is my belief that facilitated communication is an extremely useful tool which we ignore at our peril. I don't believe that it is something that can be used by everybody, and if used incorrectly it could be counter-productive. Nor do I think that everyone using it will suddenly astound us by their high levels of intelligence as Anne McDonald did. However, if somebody has something to say to us, no matter how simple, and we deny them an opportunity to try a particular method, we are denying them their voice, their right to choose, and we are controlling their life.

9 Handy tips about making it easy

This chapter has shown you that there are a variety of ways to make it easy. Whilst each method has particular advantages it will also have particular constraints. The following tips may help you when you are considering developing a particular resource:

Language

Always, always keep language as simple as possible and if you have not involved people with learning difficulties in the development of the resource, check your language with people before you begin.

Variety

Whatever the resource, vary the way the information is provided. On audiotape use music, sound effects and different voices. On posters have eye catching designs and interesting images. On videotape use music, different scenes and coloured headings, this will help people concentrate.

Limit the amount of information

Too much information can be confusing. Thus be clear when you start about how much you want to convey and be strict with yourself!

Themed resources

A strength of the posters and video was that they were on a theme such as health or leisure. It is worth producing a series of resources on the same theme so that people can pick and choose which one they want to use.

Colour coding

Each theme should have a consistent colour code. This way people will know what the resource is about without having to read. This also allows for continuity where you have more than one medium. Thus all health resources could be red, all housing blue and so on.

Quality

Since accessible information is at times more costly than printing, the temptation is to produce it on the cheap. However, money spent on glossy brochures that people do not understand is money wasted! It is likely to be far more cost effective in the long run to produce resources that people can actually use! High quality resources will also be much more effective as they will be attractive to people. In addition it gives the people who use services a clear message that we value them enough to spend money on them.

Status and Positive Images

All of the three resources tested provided information that people wanted to hear about or knew of already. This helped them feel that what they wanted to know was important. The posters and video provided attractive images of people with learning difficulties, which meant people wanted to look at them. This helped people see themselves in a more positive light and also had an impact on educating the general public too. It is also important to ensure that future resources have positive images of all people with learning difficulties including people who are black and from ethnic minority communities.

Involving people with learning difficulties

The information you produce will be greatly enhanced if you involve people in the process. This will ensure that you get your language right, provide information that people want to hear and produce positive images as a result.

Using different formats

It is possible that using a variety of different formats may help service users learn the same information in different ways. However, it is important not to bombard people with too much information at once.

10 A government health warning

In this chapter we have seen that there are many ways to make your information more accessible for people with learning difficulties. However making it is only a quarter of the battle. Using accessible information properly requires a great deal of thought and sensitivity. In the first place you need to consider whether the resource you have developed is appropriate for the individual you aim to communicate with. There's no point providing a video to someone who doesn't understand the concept of television, and it may be insulting to use symbols for someone who can read and write to a reasonable standard.

Secondly whilst this chapter has shown that accessible information works well for people with learning difficulties and is greatly appreciated by them, there are still several barriers that prevent people using them. Many of these were highlighted in the Southwark INFORM evaluations. In the next chapter I will identify some of these barriers and look at what you need to do to overcome them if you really want to take accessible information seriously.

Taking it seriously

How to use accessible information well

So far we have seen that people with learning difficulties have particular information needs in part due to the oppression and isolation they have experienced. We have also seen that people need to find information out in ways that are jargon free and go beyond the written word. In the previous chapter we saw that there are a variety of ways to inform people and using these well will take a great deal of skill.

In this chapter I will outline some of the barriers to the successful use of accessible information that emerged during the Southwark INFORM evaluation and look at ways in which we can overcome them. The evaluation also highlighted the fact that however accessible the resources people still needed some help to use them. Some suggestions are given about how to provide appropriate support. Finally I will explore ways to improve the development of accessible information in a local area and in addition improve the way information is provided.

1   Barriers to the use of accessible information

It's not that important really

The problem - One of the biggest barriers to making accessible information possible is that people don't really take it seriously enough. Other issues can seem more pressing or trendy: such as user participation, complaints, care management or consultation. Or, the day to day work of supporting someone may make things like accessible information seem an unachievable luxury. It thus gets lost behind a pile of other concerns or excuses like "well if we had the time of course we would....."

The solution - think again! As I've said good quality support is to do with giving people power. We can't do that unless people are informed and we can't inform unless it's accessible. If we really want to serve people we need to make accessible information important, or otherwise everything that is done in the name of user empowerment is completely worthless.

Resources that could not be accessed

The problem - A common theme that emerged from the evaluation of the Southwark INFORM resources was that many people did not know where the resources were kept. The audiotape questionnaire that went to support staff indicated that tapes were often kept in inaccessible places such as staff rooms and locked cupboards. Whilst the posters were often more obviously displayed; I also saw them rolled up and left on the top of cupboards in offices on more than one occasion!

The solution - Accessible information should be accessible ie available in people's bedrooms, living rooms, day centre base rooms, not locked away so people can't find it!

Staff not knowing about them

The problem - Awareness of the different media varied between services. Whilst some of the day services were heavily involved in the evaluation process, others were not; so it is possible staff there had no idea that the resources existed. It was also not uncommon for me to visit a group home and discover that staff had never heard of the resources!

The solution - Make sure people know about it! Accessible information can only work if people on the ground know it's around and are committed to its use. We thus have a responsibility to ensure staff are informed about resources and are committed to their use.

Too busy to help

The problem - As I have indicated, most people needed some support to use each resource. Several people said that staff were often so busy that they did not have the time to help. This was particularly true for the day centres.

The solution - Staff often have so many demands made on them that they are too busy to support people to use accessible information. We need to impress on staff the importance of accessible information and to ensure staff have sufficient time to support people at a pace that suits them.

Not having the right equipment

The problem - Some people did not have cassette recorders or videos. This meant they could only use the resources in day centres. This severely limited their opportunities to get at the information.

The solution - Make the equipment available! Whilst video and tape machines can be costly it is relatively easy to buy them second hand. At the very least we could buy equipment for general use that could be kept somewhere central and accessible.

Resources being forgotten about

The problem - Many of the resources were used enthusiastically when they were first produced. However, over time they were used less often, as other things took priority; and so people had less access to them later on.

The solution - Making accessible information available and supporting individuals to use it should be seen as an essential part of a staff team's role. Thus its use needs to be monitored through supervision, team meetings and staff discussions.

2   Supporting people to use it

Assisting effectively

The Southwark INFORM evaluation of the accessible resources also highlighted that people needed some help to use them.

Some people needed support to use the equipment. People needed help to turn it on, insert tapes and find their place on the tape. Although the information in the resources was fairly simple, some people still needed a member of staff to explain it a bit more. Finally people needed help following the information up. In some cases this would simply mean taking down a number, but in others it might mean helping with a phone call. As one person put it - "I'd be frightened phoning someone I don't know."

It is therefore important that people are supported to go through the process of finding the information out and then following it up. This may take several attempts before someone feels comfortable to do it alone.

Training

If accessible information is to work it needs the commitment of the people on the ground who will be supporting its use. Support staff thus need to have good training in this area.

A good training package would include the following:

• Whether they are reading a letter or passing on information about events, staff have the capability to censor the things people know about. Training should provide opportunities to consider the power staff have in the information process.

• Staff need to be aware of some of the reasons why people with learning difficulties have been so badly informed in the past and the role they could have in addressing this.

• Staff need to know how to make information accessible and how to support people to use and follow it up.

• Information training should also include developing skills in communication tools such as rebus and makaton (see Appendix).

As I stated earlier accessible information and self-advocacy are closely intertwined. Staff training should also include some time to look at what self-advocacy is and to develop the skills they need to support someone to come to their own decision or choice.

Developments in accessible information are still fairly new, however some work has been done around training. Southwark Unity self-advocacy group have developed a training resource for accessible information training (Balfe et al in publication) whilst People First of the London Boroughs are providing advice and support about accessible information through their "Make it Easy" project.

Service user training

Another way to support people with learning difficulties to use accessible information is to provide training for them. A good training package would include some of the following:

• Information is a very long word which many people don't understand. Good training should help people develop a concept of what information is and how it can help them (the work done by Oldham Disability Alliance and Fastforward referred to above may be of help).

• If people are to feel confident about asking for and using information they need opportunites to develop self-advocacy and assertiveness skills in order to state clearly their wants and needs.

• For people to take an active part in using accessible information they need an understanding of how to use equipment.

• Role plays about making telephone calls will help people overcome their nervousness about using the phone. Training is also needed to help people learn how to visit a place and take useful information away with them.

There is a need to develop some training resources in this area, although self-advocacy projects already in existence may well have training programmes that tackle some of them.

Whilst staff and service users have different training needs and some of this training can be done separately, it is also good to consider joint training. There is nothing more challenging than being faced with someone telling you how you oppress them, however unintentionally, and teaching you how you can overcome this.

3 Improving local provision

Clarifying responsibilities

Above all else services need to clarify *who* will be responsible for doing the informing. This needs clear co-ordination between services to ensure everybody knows what each other is doing.

Many local services in Southwark have over time produced their own basic information on matters specific to their service. A student on placement to Southwark INFORM spent some time with three of these services encouraging them to share information between them and think about making their information more accessible to service users who regularly drop in. This produced some tentative links between the relevant services and some useful information produced in more accessible formats. There is great potential to expand this idea and co-ordinate a range of local information centres in places that are open to service users, perhaps having the information regularly updated from a central database.

It is also possible to consider funding a specialist information resource such as the FAIR project in Edinburgh, which provides information to people with learning difficulties, their carers and support services. Alternatively, it may be worth encouraging generalist information and advice centres such as Citizen's Advice Bureaus to make their information more accessible to people with learning difficulties, so they are accessing community resources that other people use. The "total communication" project referred to in the Appendix was successful in getting their local CABs to produce information using rebus, whilst Gloucester GUIDE (an NDIP project) trained their staff to be able to respond to information enquiries from people with learning difficulties.

The broader issues highlighted in the chapter on information needs may be provided by different bodies. Many of them may be essential to the natural process of preparing people for living in the community. Thus the key informers might be support staff co-ordinated by their managers. Alternatively it could be provided by outside agencies such as adult education institutes, health organisations, or voluntary agencies who may have specialist staff. Whoever does the informing it is essential for this process to be taken slowly to ensure people are properly and adequately prepared for living in the community and fully understand the implications it has for them.

Developing initiatives

Services should take a lead in developing opportunities to provide information accessibly. The type of resource developed may however depend on the kind of information you want to produce. It is worth spending a lot of money producing high quality information when it has a long shelf life, such as complaints, user charters, general health. It is also important as it emphasises that we value people. However, when information produced changes rapidly, or is of a more personal nature, (such as information for planning meetings, personal diaries), it may be worth exploring cheaper options. This is particularly true if costs will be prohibitive otherwise. Whilst it's always good to go for the best you can, it's better to do something than nothing!

Maximising resources

Accessible information can be expensive if we wish to make it high quality. The most effective way of ensuring the majority of local information is accessible is to maximise all the local resources possible.

Purchasers of services need to be lobbied to ensure that they see accessible information as a priority and make funds available. Many statutory authorities are also obliged to produce information and they need to be convinced that they should provide this accessibly. Finally services themselves should apportion money from their budgets to produce at least some of their information in accessible formats. Where money is tight it would be worth prioritising which information is made accessible first after consulting with service users.

Local services could also co-fund major projects such as accessible information in housing or support. An excellent example of this is the five non-profit providers in Lewisham who jointly paid for a worker to be seconded to work with a user group developing workshops round a complaints video. The more we do this, the better we will be at informing people and less likely to duplicate good work.

Finally we should look to the wider community. It is likely that many places such as libraries may have the resources to provide accessible information and are just waiting to be asked! It is also worth tapping into projects that are already in an area such as. a local council taping service that may be free to disabled people or a user led video group who may be prepared to do a cheaper video.

Keeping it on the agenda

One way to keep information on the agenda would be to have an information group. This could co-ordinate developments locally, lobby organisations and funders to provide accessible information, monitor services and raise awareness and expectations. It is possible that such a group could fundraise for a communications worker who could link all the work together and provide technical advice on the development of accessible information.

4   No easy task

In this chapter I have identified some of the barriers to the effective use of accessible information and explored some ways to overcome them. I have also shown that supporting people to use accessible information is a highly skilled task and given some pointers on how to provide training opportunities for staff and people using services. Finally I have looked at ways in which we can improve information provision locally.

You will probably realise by now that taking it seriously is no easy task. It means making real commitments to people that you will make the information accessible, that you will help support them to use it effectively and you will work with other organisations to ensure that you are maximising all the resources you have locally. It also means being humble enough to admit when you've got it wrong and to learn from the people who need to use it rather than imposing pre-set ideas.

However, it is my experience that doing it properly is exciting and fun. There is nothing more satisfying than seeing people find out about things and take control of their lives. There is nothing more enjoyable than seeing people gain confidence and belief in themselves. The lessons of this chapter and indeed this book should help you in this task. Learn them well!

Conclusion - Begin it NOW

During the course of my working life, I have encountered many many instances of people with learning difficulties being oppressed and disempowered by services. The experience of working at Southwark INFORM taught me that one of the most powerful ways we can address such discrimination is to provide people with information in ways that suit them. When you know your entitlements and are surrounded by your peers who are fighting the same battle, you can gain tremendous strength to challenge the structures that oppress you.

It is my passionate belief that those of us involved in providing support to people with learning difficulties have a moral obligation to make our information accessible. Accessible information is not a luxury extra to be tacked on when we have a little time. Whilst there are many ways to counter discrimination, life without jargon should be our starting point. If we are not talking to people in ways they understand how arrogant of us to expect them to tell us what they want. If we are not making spaces for them to tell us what they want, how is it possible for us to state that we are providing flexible and responsive services?

Reading this book should have given you a flavour of the issues and I hope an enthusiasm for the subject. But my time and effort will have been completely wasted if reading it is all you do. Accessible information is not an academic subject for theoretical debate. At the end of the day it's about people. In my experience people demand action and they demand it now. So don't just sit there, get out there and DO IT NOW.

Whatever you can do or dream you can, begin it. Boldness has genius, power and magic in it. Begin it now.

Goethe

Appendix - Keep it simple!

A guide to creating accessible documents for people with learning difficulties

Figure 4 Confusing jargon

1   Introduction

The way we communicate is the essence of information giving. Use the right language, use the right medium and the message gets across. Get it wrong and people won't even know you're trying to tell them something.

Services have been very bad at communicating with people with learning difficulties in the past. Information has been passed on in long and turgid documents that are inaccessible to the average reader with little thought given to the use of symbols or pictures to help non-readers.

Fortunately times are changing and I have been very excited by the interest that I've received from colleagues in Southwark and across the country about creating accessible documents. This guide has arisen out of the work that I have been doing with individuals and agencies. It is intended as an aid to you as you work towards creating more accessible documents. It will be most beneficial to you and the people you are working towards if you treat it as such. Take what will help you and tailor your work to the individuals you work with. There are no right or wrong answers, but what you do need is a commitment to communicating with people with learning difficulties in a language they understand, using media that help not hinder.

Good luck with your documents and remember, keep them simple, keep them clear, keep them direct!

Figure 5 Using the wrong words in the wrong way

2 Thinking about language

What are you saying, why are you saying it?

Getting the language right is the most important part of creating accessible documents. Jargon and long words are obviously to be avoided, but on its own this is not enough. You need to start by thinking:

- What you want to say and why

- What a person with a learning difficulty might want to know about

- What sort of words a person with a learning difficulty is likely to know and understand

When you have thought of all these things, take your original document. Highlight the key points for yourself and make a list. If we use the above paragraphs as an example, our list would be:

- Right language

- No jargon or long words

- What you say and why

- What does person want to know

- What sort of words

How do you say it?

Having made the list, check through to make sure that everything on it is needed. Is there anything you could do without? If so get rid of it. The less crowded your document the better!

Then ask yourself, is this everything that a person with learning difficulties might need or want to know? If you really want to make your document relevant it is essential to consult user groups and individuals on what they think about a subject. If you are really pressurised for time, you may have to rely on your experience in picking out the important elements. However, you should always try and find out how much people have understood after you have written your document.

Finally, before you write anything, think about the words. What words will someone with a learning difficulty know? This is probably the hardest part of the exercise, as everyone is different. But again, you are likely to make a more meaningful document if you ask people or use your own experience.

Whilst each person will be different, you are trying to make documents that will be accessible to the widest variety of people, so there are a few general rules you should use:

- Never, never, never use professional jargon. "Social work" speak should stay in social work circles where it belongs. It is meaningless and irrelevant to people who actually use services!

- Don't abbreviate unnecessarily, people will be perplexed by terms like SELHA, JCCPG, PINs, NDIP. Always explain in full what an organisation is, and what it does, and then explain that the name can be abbreviated and what that abbreviation is.

- Don't use the third person. A document written to "you" is more friendly and more real for the reader.

- Don't use long sentences. These will be confusing. Try and keep your sentences to the simplest form, subject, verb, object.

- Avoid abstract concepts wherever possible, people will respond much better to something factual.

- Avoid double negatives, they are likely to confuse!

- Don't use small print. Always aim for 14 point at least, and try and highlight key points in bold.

- Some people find writing in capital letters easier to understand, so it is worth asking people what style they prefer.

- Always use the simplest possible word in the simplest possible way.

- Wherever possible pilot documents with people with learning difficulties to check that your language is right and the message is clear.

Following these basic rules, the example above can be written as follows:

Talking to people with learning difficulties

I want to talk to you. I must tell you so that you can understand. I will use words that you know. I will not use words that you do not understand. I will think about what I tell you. I will think what words you know. I will ask you to help me!

Figure 6 An example of simplified text

It is worth making one final comment at this point. Whilst this guide is intended for use in creating written documents, these language rules can also be applied to other media. Thus if you are preparing text for audio or videotapes, you should follow the same basic steps.

Figure 7 The wrong and the right way to tell people things

3   Thinking about symbols and pictures

Thinking about language is one thing, but if a person is unable to read or write, he or she will not be much better off even if the words are more suitable. This is where symbols and photographs come into their own. Both can be used in conjunction with text to pick out the key ideas. This will enhance the understanding of someone who can read basic English, and it will mean that non-readers can understand the message too.

What sort of symbols?

Again, I would say there are no hard and fast rules about the symbols you use. The most important thing to remember is that the system you use is relevant and consistent. This means ensuring people with learning difficulties are taught symbols that have meaning to them and are involved in the development of new ones.

Using total communication.

The total communication model practised in Somerset is a shining example of how symbols can be used extremely effectively. The system works in the following way:

1. All staff are offered a three part training programme.

2. Staff start with a one day basic course as part of their induction.

3. This is followed by a more advanced two day course open to all staff and ends with a five day advanced course that trains selected staff to be communication co-ordinators and trainers.

4. Communication co-ordinators then have the responsibility for training their colleagues.

5. Staff run communication groups in day centres and at home. These offer service users the opportunity to learn symbols that are relevant to them.

6. New symbols based on rebus are generated by service users and staff as they are needed.

7. These are fed back to the communication co-ordinators who pass them up to the speech therapists who oversee the whole programme.

This has enabled Somerset to develop a symbols system that grows and lives. People only learn symbols that they need and use, and if there is not a symbol handy they make one up. However you develop your own symbol system, you should always follow the Somerset philosophy:

> *Always use the symbol to match the need, never teach a symbol that won't be used!*

Unfortunately, there is no nationally agreed symbol system, out of preference I always use the rebus symbol system. This has many basic recognisable symbols and is used in other parts of the country. The rebus system is limited to 174 basic words, so if you base your system on it, you will still have to be prepared to develop other symbols from it. The symbols used in this guide are from the rebus glossary (van Oosterom). If you would prefer an alternative, the Makaton signing system can also be produced pictorially (Walker).

You may wish to develop your own system. However, bear in mind that if you do do this, you are likely to spend a lot of time reinventing the wheel!

However you develop your symbol system, you must be committed to developing a local strategy for co-ordination, standardisation and training of the glossary. The total communication model is an excellent way of doing this and one that I would personally recommend.

Using symbols

When symbols are known and used regularly, they become an invaluable asset for the creation of your accessible document. They are easily incorporated into written text, thus ensuring a written document is available to readers and non-readers alike.

Once you have the language right, using the symbols becomes easy. Again, you need to consider what you are communicating and why. Thus you need to choose those symbols that transmit essential parts of the information. You don't need a symbol for every word. Using symbols for the key words will be the simplest way of saying what you want to say and will be as effective as putting a symbol in for every word.

This can be illustrated using a sentence from the example above (figure 6).

> *I must tell you so that you can understand.*

Figure 8 A simplified sentence

The key words are:

I, tell, you, understand.

Thus in an accessible document the sentence would read:

I   *must tell you*   *so that you*   *can understand.*

Figure 9 A simplified sentence plus symbols

The documents plus symbols are shown below:

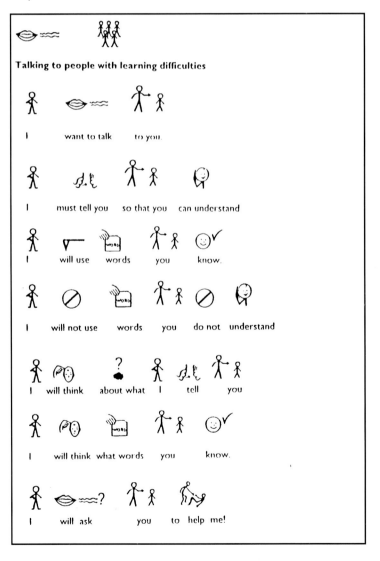

Talking to people with learning difficulties

I   want to talk   to you.

I   must tell you   so that you   can understand

I   will use   words   you   know.

I   will not use   words   you   do not understand

I   will think   about what   I   tell   you

I   will think   what words   you   know.

I   will ask   you   to help me!

Figure 10 A simplified document plus symbols

Using photographs

Photographs can also be used in documents and can sometimes convey much more information than symbols. For example, if we use the same text the photograph below clearly reflects the title:

Talking to People With Learning Difficulties

Photo by Sonay Yusuf

Figure 11 Text plus photograph

In documents about services, eg information guides, community care plans, users' charters, photographs of the relevant people and places can help the service user recognise who does what and where. A picture of a person you know will make more sense than a written name you cannot read. A photograph of a place you recognise will mean more than the written address.

Photographs will be very useful in illustrating complex documents such as complaints procedures. Simple text can be illustrated with the kind of things you can complain about, eg a broken piece of furniture, someone being pushed about. Never forget one simple photograph can convey a multitude of ideas!

Photographs can also be used in conjunction with symbols, particularly in longer documents. The symbols can be used to identify topic headings, whilst the photographs can be used to illustrate people, places or abstract concepts in the way I've just described. Southwark Consortium's User's Charter is one example of a document prepared in this way (Southwark Consortium).

Simplifying long documents in this way can make them more user friendly, but they can also make them longer! You may wish to split your more accessible document into different sections (rather like a Sunday newspaper). This will allow the person using the document more time to concentrate on one area giving them the freedom to learn at their own pace.

4   Information for YOU

When we think about accessible documents we often think about how to make the more complicated things such as Community Care Plans and Complaints Procedures easier for people to understand.

However, for many people with learning difficulties, the most important information is around the things they do, where they live, who they see and so on. For many people, key decisions about their lives are made in review and planning meetings, where the records are made in ways that are inaccessible to them.

Figure 12 The service-centred meeting

A simple way of overcoming this is to talk to the individual concerned and find out how they want such information presented. Two local Southwark services have found different ways of doing this. Brook Drive, a support agency, discovered that taping a meeting was a good way for one person to understand and remember what had happened. Toucan Employment, a supported employment agency, have produced photograph albums of service users at work. Thus the individuals concerned have a record that they can understand of what they do and who they work with.

Photographs and symbols, personal books and diaries, tapes or videos can all be used in different ways to record all kinds of personal information about jobs, review meetings, holidays, celebrations, moving house. The more involved the person becomes in the process, the more meaningful the information will be.

My book, my photos, my tape, my video ....will give me control of my life

Figure 13 The person-centred planning meeting

5 It's all very well producing them... but how are you using them?

So far this guide has shown you how you could begin to make your written documents easier for people with learning difficulties to understand. However, these documents will be totally worthless if they are just created and left on a shelf somewhere to gather dust. If you really want to make your accessible documents work, you also need to ensure the following:

- Whatever symbol system you use, it is recognisable and relevant to people with learning difficulties.

- People with learning difficulties are taught the symbols they need in order to understand the documents as they are presented.

- People with learning difficulties are regularly consulted about the language you are using and the documents you have produced. Always be prepared to take a long time to write a document so you can make use of people's comments!

- Support staff and managers at all levels of the service are given regular training in the use of symbols.

- Support staff are trained to enable people to use accessible documents.

- There is an area wide system of symbol generation and standardisation.

- There is an area wide commitment to communicating effectively with people with learning difficulties.

- You are always prepared to be flexible with your system. If something no longer works, get rid of it! If a new idea adds to people's understanding, bring it in!

If you ignore these rules, you'll have spent a lot of time, energy and resources on creating pieces of paper that look beautiful and mean nothing! If you follow them however, you will be well on your way to informing people with learning difficulties in ways that suit them.

Figure 14 Knowledge is power

Resources

1 Books and articles

Atkinson, D and Williams, F (eds) (1990) *Know me as I Am* Hodder and Stoughton

Balfe, D, Clarke, J, Flynn, C, Moffatt, V, *It's The Way That You Say It! A training pack on how to support people to find things out* Southwark Unity (in publication)

Baxter,C, Poonia, K, Ward, L, Nadirshaw, Z (1990) *Double Discrimination. Issues and Services for People with Learning Difficulties from Black and Ethnic Minority Communities* King's Fund

Brechim, A and Walmsely, J (eds) (1989) *Making Connections. Reflecting on the lives of people with learning difficulties* Hodder and Stoughton

Brown, H (1992) *An Abuse of Power* in *Community Care* 29th October 1992

Crossley, R and Mc Donald, A *Annie's Coming Out*

Cox, C and Pearson, M (1995) *Made to Care. The case for residential and village communities for people with a mental handicap* The Rannoch Trust.

Department of Health (1992) *The Health of the Nation* HMSO

Department of Health (1995) *The Health of the Nation. A strategy for people with learning disabilities* HMSO

Duffy, S (1992a) *Mutual Accord* in *Health Service Journal* 16th April 1992

Duffy, S (1992b) *Person to Person* in *Health Service Journal* 23rd April 1992

Duffy, S (1992c) *Personal Touch* in *Health Service Journal* 30th April 1992

Dowson, S (1991) *Moving to the Dance or Service Culture and Community Care* VIA

Fisher, M (1992) *The Right to Know Bill* HMSO

Greenhalgh, L (1994) *Well Aware. Improving access to health information for people with learning difficulties* NHS Executive Anglia and Oxford

Handy, C (1985) *Understanding Organisations* Penguin

HMSO (1971) *Better Services for the Mentally Handicapped*

HMSO (1990) *The NHS and Community Care Act 1990*

Lees, S (1994) *3 day user consultation, Epsom, Surrey, July 1994* NDT

Lewis, J (1995) *Give us a voice; towards equality for black and minority ethnic people with learning difficulties* Choice Press

McDonald,A (1992) *Consultation - a paper to the JCCPG* Southwark Unity (unpublished)

McMillan, I (1995) *Community Care programmes "flawed", says adviser to CNO* in   Health Service Journal March 22-28th 1995

Moffatt, V (1993a) *The Right to Know. Informing people with learning difficulties - some issues and possibilities* Southwark INFORM

Moffatt, V (1993b) *Information Directory: Information and Services for people with learning difficulties* Southwark INFORM

Moffatt, V (1993c) *Keep it Simple! A guide to creating accessible information* Southwark INFORM

Moffatt, V (1994) *What's the point of writing when I don't know how to read? Using different media to inform people with learning difficulties* Southwark INFORM

O'Farrell, J (1993) *Informing people with learning difficulties* in *Information Enables: A report of the 1993 NDIP conference* PSI

Oswin, M (1992) *Am I allowed to cry?* Souvenir Press

Parentability (1993) *What parents find helpful and unhelpful* National Childbirth Trust

People First (1992) *Oi it's my assessment!* People First

People First (1995) *Access First* People First

Rowlands, I (1992) *Information and Learning Difficulties* PSI (unpublished)

Ryan, J and Thomas, F (1980) *The politics of mental handicap* Penguin

Southwark Consortium (1993) *Southwark Consortium's User's Charter 1993* Southwark Consortium

van Oosterom, J and Devereux, K *The Rebus Glossary* Learning Development Aids

Walker, M *The Makaton Vocabulary* Makaton Vocabulary Development Project

Wertheimer, A (1987) *According to the Papers. Press reporting on people with learning difficulties* CMH

West, K (1992) *Information for people with learning difficulties - a report for the JCCPG* (unpublished)

2   Other useful products

Check it Out! a video about local leisure resources in Southwark, available from Southwark Unity, tel: 0171 403 7451.

Health, Home and Happiness a series of posters about local resources available from Southwark Unity.

It's the way that you say it! a training pack on accessible information (forthcoming from Southwark Unity).

Learning to be Mum a video about the Special Parenting Service, available from Special Parenting Service, Cornwall and Isles of Scilly Learning Disabilities NHS Trust, 4 St Clement St, Truro, Cornwall TR1 1NR, tel: 0187 274 242.

Living Your Life Pack sex education pack by Ann Craft, available from Department of Learning Difficulties, University of Nottingham Medical School, Queen's Medical Centre, Nottingham NG2 2UM.

My Choice, My Own Choice a video and teaching pack on safe sex and relationships, available from Health First! Mary Sheridan House, 15 St Thomas Street, London SE1, tel: 0171 955 4366.

Release Me a video about sex and relationships by Frances Lea, available from 971 Florence Road, Finsbury Park, London N4.

When Mum Died and When Dad Died picture books about bereavement by Sheila Hollins available from St George's Hospital Medical School, Tooting, London SW17 0RE.

3 Useful organisations

Computer technology

Gateshead Disability Information Project work with Cd-i: c/o Gateshead Council on Disability, John Haswell House, 8-9 Gladstone Terrace, Gateshead, Tyne and Wear NE8 4DY, tel: 0171 477 3558.

Oldham Disability Alliance, created a very simple computer database (also ran a user group): 4 Eldon Precint, Ashton Road, Oldham OL8 1JP, tel: 0161 628 5825.

Drama

The Lawnmowers: c/o "Them Wifies" 109 Pilgrim Street, Newcastle-upon-Tyne NE1 6QF, tel: 0191 262 4090.

Strathcona Theatre Company: Weston Street, London SE1, tel: 0171 403 9316.

Group Work and Self-Advocacy

Fastforward Pathfinders group helps people find things out through experience: 19 Buller Close, Peckham, London SE15, tel: 0171 358 0772.

People First, run a London self-advocacy project, offer support and training on issues of self-advocacy, also currently running a *Make it Easy* project: 207-213 King's Cross Road, London WC1X 9DB, tel: 0171 713 6400.

People to People, run groups for men, women and black people on sexuality and feelings: Cambridge House, 131 Camberwell Road, London SE17, tel: 0171 701 3414.

Southwark Black Users group can be contacted via: Camberwell Advocacy Office, tel: 0171 708 1408.

Southwark Unity: Rockingham Community Centre, Rockingham Estate, London SE1, tel: 0171 403 7451.

You will probably find groups like these meeting in most parts of the country.

Information

FAIR provides an information service to people with learning difficulties, their families and supporters: 25/27 West Nicolson Street, Edinburgh EH8 9DB, tel: 0131 662 1962.

Multiple Disability

CHANGE works with people with multiple disabilities and sensory impairments: 11-13 Clifton Terrace, Finsbury Park, London N4 3SR, tel: 0171 272 7774.

RNIB have a multiple disabilities team, run a specialist course and a regular newsletter: FOCUS, 224 Great Portland Street, London W1N 6AA, tel: 0171 388 1266.

SENSE works with deaf and blind children and does excellent work around sensory communication: 311 Grays Inn Road, London WC1X 8PT, tel: 0171 278 1005.

Sexuality/Sexual Abuse

Beverley Lewis House, a safe house for women with learning difficulties who have suffered sexual or physical abuse: c/o 2 Didsbury Close, Melbourne Road, London E6, tel: 0181 522 0675.

NAPSAC is an umbrella organisation providing information about different groups and a regular newsletter: Department of Learning Difficulties, University of Nottingham Medical School, Queen's Medical Centre, Nottingham NG2 2UM.

Respond offers counselling to victims of abuse: 24–32 Stephenson Way, London NW1 2HD, tel: 0171 383 0700

Audiotaping

There are many organisations that provide taping services. These are just a few of them. They differ in the variety of services they can offer, quality and price.

Disabilities Resources Team: Bedford House, 125-133 Camden High Street, London NW1 7JR, tel: 0171 482 5299.

Gateshead AIRS Project: Gateshead Central Library, Prince Consort Road, Gateshead, Tyne and Wear NE8 4LN, tel: 0191 477 3478.

T.N.E.L National Recording Centre: 10 Browning Road, Station Road Industrial Estate, Heathfield, East Sussex TN21 8DB, tel: 0014 358 6610.

RNIB: 224 Great Portland Street, London WIN 6AA, tel: O171 388 1266.

Photography

Photography projects are fairly thin on the ground! Sadly the Blackfriars Photography Project has closed due to lack of funds. The following organisations and people may be able to help.

Action Space: 336 Brixton Road, Brixton, London SW9, tel: 0171 274 2847. This project employs photography, art and drama tutors.

Melanie Jackson: c/o 268 Columbia Road, London E2 7RN. Melanie was the tutor on the *Health, Home and Happiness* project. She is a freelance worker and can be contacted via this address.

Shape London, tel: 0171 960 9660. Shape may have information on projects.

London Disability Arts Forum: The Diorama, Peto Place, London NW1, tel and minicom: 0171 935 5588. LDAF may have information on projects.

Video

The video business is booming at present. The following is a small selection:

First Field Video for Arts and Education: 77 Royal College Street, London NW1 OSE, tel: 0171 911 0338.

"Them Wifies": 109 Pilgrim Street, Newcastle-upon-Tyne NE1 6QF, tel: 0191 262 4090.

Fastforward Project: Mental Health Media Resource Council, 365 Holloway Road, London N7 PA, tel: 0171 700 0100 ext 272. This project is researching the use of videos, and is in contact with over 200 organisations.

The Grange Video Project is a user-led project creating videos for themselves. This enterprising group has interviewed several celebrities as well as making videos on sport etc: The Grange, 12 - 13 Grange Road, London SE1 3BE, tel: 0171 237 9518.

Entelechy create high quality videos on commission: contact David Slater, Mulberry Centre 15 Amersham Vale, London SE1 6LE.

Other useful contacts

People First are running a three year project *Make it Easy* which will be developing accessible information resources and pushing the message: contact Wendy at People First, Instrument House, 207-215 King's Cross Road, London WC1X 9DB, tel: 0171 713 6400

Printed by HMSO Scotland 3/96 (120320)